Inspirational Thoughts

VOLUME TWO

A Compilation of wonderful quotations for your personal growth.

Tycho Photiou

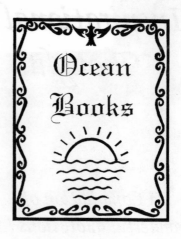

Ocean Books
18 Pentrich Avenue,
Enfield, Middlesex.
EN1 4LZ.
Tel (020) 8350 9600

*Those who are awake
live in a state of
constant amazement.*
THE BUDDHA

The sources of quotations in this book are many and varied - there are quotations from various religious texts, particularly Buddhism and Christianity, and there are many quotations from wise men and women through the centuries including, and up to, the present day.

Some of the relatively modern sources are acknowledged in the bibliography. Whilst the publisher has made every effort to obtain permission for the quotations wherever appropriate, this may not have been possible in every case.

We would therefore like to thank everyone who provided the wonderful and rich teachings that you will find within these pages, and accept our apologies if any modern sources have not been adequately acknowledged.

1st Edition - Published 2001

Printed in Great Britain by
Redwood Books Ltd, Kennet Way, Trowbridge,
Wiltshire, BA14 8RN.

This will be a better world
when the power of love
replaces the love of power.

ANONYMOUS

Contents

*The only way to bring peace
to the earth is to learn
to make our own
life peaceful.*

THE BUDDHA

Life
and
Death

*On no subject are our ideas
more warped and pitiable
than on death.*

JOHN MUIR

*It is impossible that
anything so natural, so
necessary, and so universal
as death, should ever have
been designed
by providence as an
evil to mankind.*

JONATHAN SWIFT

We live in a
beautifully balanced system
in which death is a part of
everything that lives.
The pain of our personal
loss is ours; within
the greater whole,
nothing is lost.

KAREN CASEY / MARTHA VANCEBURG

As soon as man is born
he begins to die.

ANONYMOUS

*The price we pay
for living is dying,
The price we pay
for loving is grief.*

ANDREA PHOTIOU

*Unless you fully accept
the inevitability of death,
it's hard to enjoy this
interval called life.*

JOHN-ROGER/PETER MCWILLIAMS

*Everything that has a
beginning has an ending.
Make your peace with that
and all will be well.*

THE BUDDHA

*Man fools himself.
He prays for a long life,
and he fears old age.*

CHINESE PROVERB

9

The spirit kills not,
nor is it killed.
It was not born;
it will never die.
Nor once having been,
can it ever cease to be:
Unborn, Eternal, Ever-
enduring, yet most ancient,
the Spirit dies not when
the body is dead.....
Knowing the Spirit as such,
thou hast no cause
to grieve.

Bhagavad Geeta.

Dear death,
were you not there,
what to life
would I compare?
How could I measure time,
and appreciate what is mine?
But existing as you do,
I compare sweet life
with you, like a glow
against the night,
you keep life in my sight.

ANDREA PHOTIOU.

Energy cannot be created or destroyed only transformed. Therefore you have no need to fear death, just see it as a transformation from the physical to the spiritual.

THOMAS ALLEN

The fear of death is more to be dreaded than death itself.

PUBLILIUS SYRUS

If there's something to fear,
it's the feeling of
fear on its own.
If there's something to
dread, it's the dread that
the feeling has grown.

ANDREA PHOTIOU

People living deeply have
no fear of death.

ANAIS NIN

*Beyond any body of
evidence about ageing and
how to prevent it,
the single most important
factor is that you make
something creative
from your existence.*
DR. DEEPAK CHOPRA

*No wise man ever wished
to be younger.*
JONATHAN SWIFT

The greatest threat to life
and health is having
nothing to live for.
DR. DEEPAK CHOPRA

You don't get to choose
how you're going
to die, or when.
You can only decide how
you are going to live.
Now.
JOAN BAEZ

One must not lose desires.
They are mighty stimulants
to creativity, to love
and to long life.
ALEXANDER BOGOMOLETE

If we expire when we die,
shouldn't we inspire
while we live.
GEORGE GOLDTRAP

At the moment of death.....
.....there arises before man's
mind, the vision of his life
to come, a vision regulated
by his impressions of
his past deeds.

HINDUISM, SRIMAD, BHAGAVATAM 11.15

To be or not to be,
that is the question.........
for in that sleep of death
what dreams may come,
when we have shuffled off
this mortal coil....

WILLIAM SHAKESPEARE

Know
Thyself

*To be curious of
that which is not
my concern, while I am
in ignorance of my own self,
would be ridiculous.*

PLATO

*Knowing others
is knowledge;
Knowing oneself is wisdom.*

THE BUDDHA

*Self-reflection is
the school of wisdom.*

BALTASAR GRACIAN

*There are infinite ways
to discover your true being,
but love holds
the brightest torch.*

TYCHO

*We are all in this
classroom called earth trying
to discover something - the
ultimate, and we are all
looking for it externally.
Where is it?
If we only turn our
direction back upon
ourselves, we will discover,
it's right here
where I am.*

LESTER LEVENSON

*If you can't find the truth
right where you are,
where else do you think
you will find it?*

THE BUDDHA

*Nowhere can man find a
calmer or more untroubled
haven than in his own soul.*

MARCUS AURELIUS

You are both a finite earthly
being, and an infinite soul
of great spiritual dimension.
You are the drop of water
and the wave.
You direct yourself and
you are directed.

CAROL ADRIENNE

You are not a human being having a spiritual experience. You are a spiritual being having a human experience.

WAYNE DYER

I haven't got a soul, I am a soul.

ANONYMOUS

A person who knows himself as spirit never loses sight of the experiencer in the midst of experience.

DR DEEPAK CHOPRA

If you do not go within, you go without.

NEALE DONALD WALSCH

*People who practice
meditation begin to discover
a deeper aspect of life and
an ease, a joy, a happiness
which is not dependent
upon outer circumstances.*
F. W. WHITING

*Internal conflicts
create external ones.*
ANONYMOUS

*My true relationship is my
relationship with myself
- all others are
simply mirrors of it.*

SHAKTI GAWAIN

*All the loveliness of nature
is but a reflection of that
which is within our souls.*

HARI PRASAD SHASTRI

*He that beholds must be
akin to that which he
beholds. Never can the soul
see beauty unless she has
become beautiful.*

*Beauty is in
the eye of the beholder.*
PROVERB

.....the part of the object's
beauty that stands out to
each person reflects
back qualities he or she
already possesses.

JAMES REDFIELD/CAROL ADRIENNE

We are all One

The most important
characteristic of the
Eastern world view - one
could almost say the essence
of it - is the awareness of
the unity and mutual
interrelation of all
things and events.

FRITJOF CAPRA

Your own Self
lives in the heart of all.

THE UPANISHAD

That which fills
the universe I regard
as my body,
and that which directs
the universe I see as
my own nature.

CHANG-TZU

Without going outside,
you may know the
whole world.

LAO TZU

*You are not enclosed
within your bodies,
nor confined to
houses or fields.
That which is you dwells
above the mountain
and roves with the wind.*

KAHLIL GIBRAN

*If you wish to know the
divine, feel the wind on your
face and the warm sun
on your hand.*

THE BUDDHA

34

*All your suffering
is rooted in one error.
You believe that you live in
the world, when in fact the
world lives in you.*

ANONYMOUS

*He experiences himself,
his thoughts and feelings
as something separated from
the rest - a kind of optical
delusion of consciousness.*

ALBERT EINSTEIN

I am you.
The light of consciousness
is one, but it is shone
through different
instruments which gives the
illusion of separateness.
Dr. Katherine Watson.

There is but one mind,
every man is an inlet to
that one mind....
Ralph Waldo Emerson

You are all the fruits
of one tree and the leaves
of one branch.

BAHA'I FAITH.

The physical world is just
a mirror of a
deeper intelligence.
Intelligence is the
invisible organiser of
all matter and energy.

DR. DEEPAK CHOPRA

*Love is the guiding force
which enables us to see the
unity in all things.*

TYCHO

*We are not isolated beings
but live in a world that is a
holistic continuum. The way
we think affects not only us,
but other people too.*

BILL ANDERTON

*You can never be lonely if
you experience your
aloneness as all-oneness.*

TYCHO

*If you can stop thinking
for one moment you will
go through the most
tremendous experience there
is - that you are the totality
of this universe in
your beingness.*

LESTER LEVENSON

...Individuality itself seemed to dissolve and fade away into boundless being, and this is not a confused state but the clearest of the clear, the surest of the sure, utterly beyond words, where death was almost a laughable impossibility....

TENNYSON

Everything that is, is alive.

MICHAEL HARNER

To see a world in a grain of sand and a heaven in a wild flower, hold infinity in the palm of your hand, and eternity in an hour.

WILLIAM BLAKE

National Borders are a Human Construct

If only we could all transcend the attachment to the label of "my country" and replace it with a devotion for not only our country but for the whole of humanity, then the world would become one family and earthly conflict would cease.

TYCHO

It is not for him to pride
himself for loving his own
country, but rather for him
to love the whole world.
The earth is but
one country, and mankind
its citizens.

BAHA'I FAITH - GLEANINGS 117

Can there be any human
activity more insane than to
kill another human being
because he happened to
be born the other side
of the border?

TYCHO

45

Falsely seeing the world as one of separate, fragmented entities is what causes antagonism, greed, and inevitably suffering.

THE BUDDHA

Under the light of consciousness there is no east and west, only unity.

DR. KATHERINE WATSON

*See all living beings on
this planet as one;
fragmentation and division
are the main problems in our
outlook towards ourselves,
our family and
our planetary society.*
TYCHO

Imagine there's no countries,
it isn't hard to do.
Nothing to kill or die for,
and no religion too.
Imagine all the people living
life in peace......

JOHN LENNON

Religion
and
Spirituality

.....if there is one
holy person in a village,
the whole village reaps the
benefit of his or her
enlightenment.

JAMES REDFIELD/CAROL ADRIENNE

Life is but a dream pouring
forth from a stream we
sometimes call God or
universal consciousness.

THOMAS ALLEN

Tests are benefits from God, for which we should thank him. Grief and sorrow do not come to us by chance, they are sent to us for our own perfecting.

BAHA'I FAITH

All things that you ask in prayer, while believing, you shall receive.

JESUS CHRIST

Prayer indeed is good,
but while calling on the
Gods a man should himself
lend a hand.

HIPPOCRATES

All things are possible to
he who believes.

JESUS CHRIST

Well if God can't inspire
you, who in hell can?

NEALE DONALD WALSH

For those who believe,
no proof is necessary,
For those who don't
believe, no proof is possible.
JOHN AND LYN ST. CLAIR THOMAS

Religion is for people who
are scared of going to Hell;
Spirituality is for people
who have been there!
BEECHY COLCLOUGH

*True religion is to cleanse
oneself with pure thoughts,
pure words, and pure deeds.*

ZOROASTRIANISM

*Organised religion sometimes
pulls us away from the
spiritual part of who we are.*

SUSAN JEFFERS

Religion became corrupted when leaders where assigned to explain God's will to people instead of showing them how to find this direction within themselves.

JAMES REDFIELD/CAROL ADRIENNE

True spirituality is beyond rule and ritual, or attachment to labels and doctrine.

TYCHO

You don't know you've been
entrapped until you
have been set free.

EARL NIGHTINGALE

It wasn't sin that was
born on the day when Eve
picked an apple; what was
born on that day was a
splendid virtue called
disobedience.

ORIANA FALLACI

Live as lamps to yourselves,
as refuges to yourselves,
with no other refuges.

THE BUDDHA

If you have faith,
let it be not blind faith;
let it be a faith that
glows with wisdom.

ANDREA PHOTIOU

There is the most interesting
resemblance between
the effects of stimulants,
narcotics or hypnotic
control and blind
unreasoning faith.
The latter also
benumbs and paralyses
judgement and reason.

HENRY LINDLAHR

*Faith without doubt
is folly!*
THOMAS ALLEN

*Do not blindly believe
what others say.
See for yourself what
brings contentment,
clarity, and peace.
That is the path for
you to follow.*
THE BUDDHA

*Believe those who are
seeking the truth;
Doubt those who find it.*
ANDRE GIDE

*The fear of God
is the end of wisdom.*
TYCHO

With an open mind,
you will be open-hearted.
Being open-hearted,
you will act royally.
Being royal, you will
attain the divine.

LAO TZU

Sexuality
and
Spirituality

Many people still suffer from the mistaken idea that spiritual energy and sexual energy are opposite, instead of recognising that they are the same force.

SHAKTI GAWAIN

Sexual exchange with a
loving partner promotes
feelings of well-being and
builds self-esteem.

JUDITH SACHS

Spirituality must also be
sensuous, because a
spiritual person is one who
lives fully in the moment,
which means living fully
in the body.

DR. DEEPAK CHOPRA

Our families, peers, society and religious organisations only aid us in attempting to suppress, control or exploit what is natural.

SHAKTI GAWAIN

Negative conditioning doesn't stop you from engaging in the sex act; it just stops you enjoying it!

TYCHO

I find it hard to believe that the vast, incredible Intelligence that created this entire Universe is only an old man sitting on a cloud above the planet Earth ......watching my genitals!

LOUISE L. HAY

*With love being an all
engulfing essence of so many
aspects of living well,
the part that sex plays in it
should be akin to all
creative expressions.*

ANDREA PHOTIOU.

Fear and Worry or Love and Trust?

There is the path of fear
and the path of love.
Which will you follow?

THE BUDDHA

Fear is the energy which
contracts, closes down,
draws in, runs, hides,
hoards, harms.
Love is the energy which
expands, opens up, sends
out, stays, reveals,
shares, heals.

NEALE DONALD WALSCH

*Fear is a perversion of the
great law of faith;
it is faith in evil.*

HENRY LINDLAHR

*What you fear most is what
will most plague you.
Fear will draw it
to you like a magnet.*

NEALE DONALD WALSCH

*Our own worst enemy
cannot harm us as much as
our unwise thoughts.
No one can help us as
much as our own
compassionate thoughts.*

THE BUDDHA

*I will judge no-one today.
I would rather be cheated
once or twice than live my
whole life in fear
and suspicion.*

MIKE LIPKIN

Remember that the best
relationship is one
where your love for each
other is greater than your
need for each other.
IAN MCDERMOTT / JOSEPH O CONNOR

Masters are those who
have chosen only love
in every instance,
in every moment.
NEALE DONALD WALSCH

To love is to admire
with the heart:
To admire is to love
with the mind.
ANONYMOUS

Love in the past
is only a memory.
Love in the future
is a fantasy.
Only here and now
can we truly love.
THE BUDDHA

73

The mind thinks;
Love links.
CHRISTOPHER GILMORE

All children are born equal
but when they arrive at the
door of adulthood each is
measured by their capacity
to love their fellow man.
ANDREA PHOTIOU

74

Let it go

Let it be

In life what sometimes appears to be the end is really a new beginning.

THOMAS ALLEN

There can be no rainbow without a cloud or storm.

ANONYMOUS

If you go beyond the clouds, there is always sunshine.

PROVERB

*Anxiety does not empty
tomorrow of its sorrows
- it only empties today
of its strength.*
ANONYMOUS

*The longer you dwell
on your misfortunes,
the greater is their power
to hurt you.*
VOLTAIRE

*To be stressed causes ones
head to be hot not cool, ones
stomach to be churning not
calm, and ones aura to
diminish not radiate.*

ANDREA PHOTIOU

*Tiredness is not caused by
what the body does,
it is caused by the state of
the body while it does it.*

TYCHO

Praise and blame, gain and loss, pleasure and sorrow come and go like the wind. To be happy, rest like a great tree in the midst of them all.

THE BUDDHA

It is fine to have desires, what we need is to transcend our attachment to those desires.

TYCHO

*Desire is the
beginning of all creation.
Attachment to desire
is what causes a
person to suffer.*

THOMAS ALLEN

*The radical approach
is to enjoy more.
If you enjoy everything
you get attached to nothing,
because you pass from one
enjoyment to another.*

ROBERTO ASSIAGILIO

*Our attachments are
inversely proportional to
our capacity to enjoy.*
PIERO FERRUCCI

*In times of difficulty
take refuge in
compassion and truth.*
THE BUDDHA

Enjoyment is
gratuitous and pure.
Attachment is
greedy and expectant.
Enjoyment lives in the now.
Attachment lives in the
past or projects itself
into the future.
Enjoyment is open
to experience.
Attachment wants
to program it.

PIERO FERRUCCI

The man,
who casting off
all desires, lives free
from attachment, who is
free from egoism and from
the feelings that this or
that is mine, obtains
tranquillity.

BHAGAVAD GITA 2.71

Time
and the
Timeless

Time is the movement of thought. Both past and future are born in the imagination; only the present, which is awareness, is real and eternal.

DEEPAK CHOPRA

If you take care of each moment, you will take care of all time.

THE BUDDHA

The best way to prepare for
any moment in the future
is to be fully conscious
in the present.
DEEPAK CHOPRA

Contrary to popular opinion,
the whole of your life is
not in front of you......
it is here right now.
THOMAS ALLEN

*There is only one time when
it is essential to awaken.
That time is now.*
THE BUDDHA

*As you walk and eat and
travel, be where you are.
Otherwise you will miss
most of your life.*
THE BUDDHA

Look to this day,
for yesterday is but a dream
and tomorrow is
only a vision.
But today well lived makes
every yesterday a dream of
happiness and every
tomorrow a vision of hope.

SANSKRIT PROVERB

Love Yourself Too

God asks only that
you include yourself
among those you love.
NEALE DONALD WALSH

You did what you knew
how to do, and when you
knew better, you did better.
MAYA ANGELOU

We can pardon everyone's
mistakes but our own.
ANONYMOUS

90

*A person with a confident
self-image always sits,
stands and walks with
a healthier posture
than someone with an
inferiority complex.*

TYCHO

*What makes for a straighter
spine: vitamin D, milk
or self-esteem?*

DR. DEEPAK CHOPRA

Go first to your highest thought about yourself. Imagine the you that you would be if you lived that thought every day.

NEALE DONALD WALSH

If you're unable to forgive yourself, then ask God to do it for you.

THOMAS ALLEN

92

Keep Smiling

You've reached middle age
when all you exercise
is caution.

ANONYMOUS

You can tell your in your
golden years by all the
silver in your hair.

ANONYMOUS

Today is the tomorrow you
worried about yesterday.

ANONYMOUS

Something you think does
you good, does you more
good than something that
does do you good.

ANONYMOUS

A woman spends half her
marriage moulding her man
as she wants him,
and half wishing he was the
man she first met.

ANONYMOUS

*Live every day as if it
were your last....
one day you'll be right.*
ANONYMOUS

*If you worry, you die,
if you don't worry you die.
So, why worry?*
ANONYMOUS

Towards True Success

*Far away in the sunshine
are my highest aspirations.
I may not reach them,
but I can look up and see
their beauty, believe in
them, and try to follow
where they lead.*

ANONYMOUS

A successful person is one who is able to fulfil his potential by listening to the wisdom of his own heart.

TYCHO

If you don't enjoy what you have, how could you be happier with more?

ANONYMOUS

*Success is
getting what you want.
Happiness is
wanting what you get.*

HARRY LORRAYNE

*It is what we value,
not what we have
- that makes us rich.*

ANONYMOUS

100

*Beware the man who
knows the price of
everything and
the value of nothing.*

ANONYMOUS

*It's becoming clear that the
ladder to success has become
the ladder to distress.*

SUSAN JEFFERS

O shrewd businessman, do
only profitable business:
deal only in that commodity
which shall accompany
you after death.
SIKHIST PROVERB

When wishes are few,
the heart is happy.
When desire ends,
there is peace.
THE BUDDHA

No man is a failure who
is enjoying life.
WILLIAM FEATHER

What is fulfilling
is not dependent
on the ever changing
circumstances of life.
MARJOLEIN WOLF

There are two ways to
become financially wealthy:
To earn more than enough to
satisfy all your desires,
or to desire less than what
you can afford.

TYCHO

When we set our intention
for what we desire,
we achieve it usually only
when we have released
our need to have it.

CAROL ADRIENNE

Strange as it may seem,
life becomes serene and
enjoyable precisely when
selfish pleasure and personal
success are no longer
the guiding goals.

MIHALY CSIKSZENTMIHALY

When we learn
how to truly give,
we will know
how to truly live.

TYCHO

A man who does great good
but talks not of it,
is on the way to perfection.
BAHA'I FAITH

Two qualities inherent
in consciousness are
attention and intention.
Attention energises and
intention transforms.
DR. DEEPAK CHOPRA

*If you always do
what you've always done;
you'll always get
what you've always got.*

ANONYMOUS.

*Insanity is repeating the
same mistakes and expecting
different results.*

ANONYMOUS.

We are Unlimited Beings

*The ancients have declared
since time immemorial the
unlimited potential which
lies within each and every
one of us, but is buried
under concepts of limitation.*

LESTER LEVENSON

To say we are
"unlimited beings"
is not only saying that we
are beings of great
potential, it is saying that
we are beings of <u>infinite</u>
potential.

TYCHO

*Your perception of ultimate
reality is more limited
than you thought,
and truth is more unlimited
than you can imagine.*

NEALE DONALD WALSCH

*Life is a process of
constant transformation,
not decline, and therefore is
full of potential for
unlimited growth.*

DR DEEPAK CHOPRA

*You have no limits except
those you hold onto
in your mind.
When you let go of these
limits, you can have, do, or
be, whatever you desire.*

LESTER LEVENSON

*What lies behind us and
what lies before us,
are tiny matters compared
to what lies within us.*

RALPH WALDO EMERSON

*Your limitations are created
by what you believe your
limitations are.*

TYCHO

*Be afraid of nothing.
You have within you:
All wisdom, all power, all
strength, all understanding.*

EILEEN CADDY

Unless you try to do something beyond what you have already mastered you will never grow.

ANONYMOUS

Only those who will risk going too far can possibly find out how far one can go.

T. S. ELLIOT

*Some of you are walking in
wakefulness, and some of
you are sleepwalking.
Yet all of you are creating
your own reality -
creating not discovering.*

NEALE DONALD WALSCH

*The creative intelligence
and energy of the universe
is the fundamental
source of everything.
Once we connect with this
and surrender to it,
everything is ours.*

SHAKTI GAWAIN

*Neither a lofty degree of intelligence nor imagination nor both together go to the making of a genius.
Love, love, love, that is the soul of genius.*

ARMADIUS MOZART

True creativity comes out of stillness.

DR CATHERINE WATSON

To make ethical
decisions use your heart;
What arises from your mind
when you rationalise
are not truths but
rational-lies.

TYCHO

There are many things in life
that will catch your eye, but
only a few will catch your
heart....pursue those.

ANONYMOUS

118

The kingdom of heaven is within you, and whoever knows himself shall find it. And, having found it, you shall know yourselves that you are in God and God is in you. And you are the kingdom of God.

JESUS CHRIST

BIBLIOGRAPHY

Ageless body, timeless mind - Deepak Chopra. Published by Rider 1993.

Living in the Light - Shakti Gawain. Published by Eden Grove Editions.

Staying on the path - Dr. Wayne W. Dyer. Published by Hay House, Inc.

The Celestine Prophecy, An adventure - James Redfield. Published by Bantam books.

The Celestine Prophecy, An experiential guide - James Redfield and Carol Adrienne. Published by Bantam books.

The purpose of your life - Carol Adrienne. Published by Thorsons.

Feel the fear and do it anyway - Susan Jeffers. Published by Arrow books limited.

End the struggle and dance with life - Susan Jeffers. Published by Coronet Books limited.

Yoga - Hari Prasad Shastri. Published by W& G Foyle Ltd.

Being Oneself - F. W. Whiting. Published by The school of meditation.

The Healing Power Of Sex - Judith Sachs. Published by Prentice Hall (US only).

A guide for the advanced soul - Susan Hayward. Published by In-tune books.

Eyes of the beholder - John and Lyn St. Clair-Thomas/Steven Shackel. Published by Angel Publications.

The Dawn of change - Eileen Caddy. Published by The Findhorn press.

God spoke to me - Eileen Caddy. Published by The Findhorn press.

Introducing NLP - Joseph O'Connor and John Seymour. Published by Thorsons.

You can't afford the luxury of a negative thought - John-Roger and Peter McWilliams. Published by Thorsons.

The Philosophy of Natural Therapeutics - Henry Lindlahr. Published by the C.W. Daniel Company.

The Tao of physics - Fritjof Capra. Published by Flamingo.

Life after life - Raymond A. Moody Jr. M.D. Published by Bantam books.

The promise of a new day - Karen Casey and Martha Vanceburg. Published by Hazelden Meditation series.

You can Heal your life - Louise L. Hay. Published by Eden Grove Editions.

The Prophet - Kahlil Gibran. Published by Penguin Arkana.

The way of the Shaman - Michael Harner. Published by Thorsons.

Soul Centred Education - Christopher Gilmore. Published by Dovetales. Tel - 01270 652 392.

Meditations with God - Neale Donald Walsch. Published by Hodder and Staughton.

What we may be - Piero Ferrucci. Published by Thorsons

Manifest your Destiny - Wayne Dyer. Published by Thorsons.

Live as if it is your last day,
dream as if you're going
to live forever.
JAMES DEAN

*The best way to predict the
future is to create it.*

ANONYMOUS